Pg.193

DARING WOMEN

# ~25~
# WOMEN
## ~ WHO ~
# FOUGHT BACK

by Jill Sherman

COMPASS POINT BOOKS
a capstone imprint

Compass Point Books are published by Capstone Press
1710 Roe Crest Drive, North Mankato, Minnesota 56003
www.mycapstone.com

**Library of Congress Cataloging-in-Publication Data**
Library of Congress Cataloging-in-Publication data is available on the Library of Congress website.

ISBN 978-0-7565-5850-5 (hardback)
ISBN 978-0-7565-5867-3 (paperback)
ISBN 978-0-7565-5855-0 (eBook PDF)

**Editorial Credits**
Anna Butzer, editor; Russell Griesmer, designer; Jennifer Bergstrom, production artist;
Svetlana Zhurkin, media researcher; Laura Manthe, production specialist

**Photo Credits**
AP Images: 14, Frank C. Curtin, 11, Scanpix/Cornelius Poppe, cover; Franklin D. Roosevelt Presidential Library and Museum, 9; Getty Images: Anthony Barboza, 23, Curran/Steve Jennings, 27, Popperfoto/United News, 45, Robin Marchant, 32, The LIFE Images Collection/Don Cravens, 37; Library of Congress, 7, 35; NARA: Franklin D. Roosevelt Library, 5; Newscom: EFE/Giorgio Viera, 47, picture alliance/EuropaNewswire/Luiz Rampelotto, 30, Reuters/Aaron Josefczyk, 25, Sipa Press/Benedicte Desrus, 43, Sipa USA/Lionel Hahn, 16, Sipa USA/Luiz Rampelotto, 51, Sipa/Anthony Behar, 49, Sipa/Lido, 21, Zuma Press/Aftonbladet, 28, Zuma Press/Heiko Junge, 58, Zuma Press/Stefan Rousseau, 54; Shutterstock: Joseph Sohm, 18, lev radin, 56, stocklight, 39; Wikimedia, 41

Design Elements by Shutterstock

Printed in the United States of America.
PA017

# TABLE OF CONTENTS

# INTRODUCTION

"All human beings are born free and equal in dignity and rights."

Those words begin the Universal Declaration of Human Rights, signed by the members of the United Nations in 1948. But words alone do not make people free and equal.

Throughout history, the fight for justice and equality has been carried on by brave women all over the world. Their stories remind us to use our minds, voices, talents, and resources to fight for freedom and equality for everyone, every day.

The U.S. Constitution does not guarantee equal rights based on gender. Starting in the 1970s and for decades afterward, women fought for a constitutional amendment to guarantee equal rights to all women, but the efforts did not succeed.

*Eleanor Roosevelt said her role in drafting the Universal Delcaration of Human Rights was her greatest achievement.*

# Chapter 1

# WOMEN WHO FOUNDED MOVEMENTS

From the suffragists to modern-day feminists, women have fought to end discrimination. Protests that began with just a few women often grew into national movements that could not be overlooked by people in power. These women understood that they were more powerful together. Their marches, conventions, and boycotts changed the nation.

## Susan B. Anthony
### (1820–1906)

The gavel pounded. The verdict came down: guilty. Judge Ward Hunt declared that Susan B. Anthony had committed a crime when she voted in the presidential election. He ordered her to pay a $100 fine.

*Susan B. Anthony, 1891*

Anthony did not stand silent when the verdict was read. She objected to "laws made by men, under a government of men, interpreted by men and for the benefit of men." She told Judge Hunt, "The only chance women have for justice in this country is to violate the law, as I have done, and as I shall continue to do."

In standing up for her right to vote, Anthony was carrying on a family tradition. She grew up in a Quaker family. Like many Quakers, her family worked to support social causes such as ending slavery and the temperance movement. Temperance sought to limit or end the sale of alcohol.

Anthony worked as a teacher from 1839 to 1849. During that time, she remained involved in the temperance movement. She attended a temperance rally in Albany, New York, in 1852. But because women weren't allowed to speak at rallies, she was denied the opportunity to speak. Soon after, Anthony formed the Woman's State Temperance Society of New York.

Anthony's experience at the New York rally stayed with her. She came to believe that no one would take women in politics seriously unless they had the right to vote. Anthony teamed up with fellow activist Elizabeth Cady Stanton to form the National Woman Suffrage Association in 1869.

Anthony had long supported both the abolition of slavery and equal rights for African Americans. After the Civil War, the 15th Amendment to the U.S. Constitution gave the vote to black men, but not to women of any color. Because of this, Anthony opposed the amendment. She believed that its passage would set back the women's suffrage movement.

Anthony was tireless in her work for

women's rights. She started petitions to help women gain the right to own property and to vote. She traveled all around the country giving speeches to persuade people to support women's right to vote.

Anthony never gave up her fight for women's rights, even meeting with President Theodore Roosevelt in 1905 to lobby for a constitutional amendment. Anthony died in 1906 and was buried in Rochester, New York. It would take another 14 years before the 19th Amendment was passed, finally giving women the right to vote. Each year, women honor Anthony's commitment to women's suffrage on Election Day. They visit her grave to leave behind their "I Voted" stickers.

## Eleanor Roosevelt
### (1884–1962)

When Eleanor Roosevelt disagreed with her husband, she picked up a pen and

*Eleanor Roosevelt, 1936*

wrote about it. Not in a diary or a letter left on the kitchen table, but in her newspaper column, seen by millions of Americans. Her husband was President Franklin Delano Roosevelt. But that did not stop Eleanor from speaking up when she believed his policies would not serve the American people. Alongside her husband, she used her powerful platform to fight for human rights and human dignity.

Anna Eleanor Roosevelt was born in New York City on October 11, 1884. Her mother and brother died of a bacterial disease called diphtheria when Eleanor was eight. Her father died in a mental institution two years later. Described as the ugly duckling of her family, Eleanor occasionally suffered from periods of depression.

Eleanor married Franklin Delano Roosevelt in 1905. Franklin was diagnosed with polio in 1921. Even though polio led to the loss of the use of his legs, Eleanor encouraged him to stay in politics.

As first lady, Eleanor publicly supported the equal treatment of African American citizens. She repeatedly broke tradition by befriending and supporting black people. She arranged for African American singer Marian Anderson to sing at a number of events.

In 1939 Anderson was beginning to be a very popular singer and the crowds that gathered to see her were large. The team that organized Anderson's concerts asked the Daughters of the American Revolution (DAR) to use the Constitution Hall in Washington, D.C., as the arena for Anderson's next show because it could hold a large number of people. But because the DAR enforced segregation, only white performers were allowed on the stage. Eleanor did not agree with the DAR's decision. She arranged for Anderson to sing at the Lincoln Memorial. And she resigned from the DAR over their segregation policy after being a member for six years. Eleanor explained that her resignation was a rejection of segregation.

During World War II, she encouraged women to take up factory jobs and supported the work of black pilots in the military.

During her husband's four terms as president, she used her unique platform to argue for a better life for all human beings.

After Franklin died in 1945, Eleanor continued her work as a public and political figure. She was appointed chairwoman of the United Nations Commission on Human Rights. In that position, she worked to draft the Universal Declaration of Human Rights. It was published in 1948. The declaration was a response to the genocide committed against the Jews by the Nazis in World War II. It set the standards for treating all humans with dignity and has been translated into almost every written language on Earth.

Eleanor Roosevelt was one of the most influential women of the 20th century.

*Pauli Murray, 1971*

# Pauli Murray
## (1910–1985)

In the early 1900s, the school for African American children in Durham, North Carolina, sat on bare clay. In winter, wind howled through the chinks in its rickety planks. In summer, paint peeled off the building. The school for white children was made of brick. It was surrounded by a green lawn, and children played on swing sets and slides. Growing up in Durham, Anna Pauline (Pauli) Murray felt the painful contrast between the schools. She spent her life fighting against these unequal conditions.

In 1939 Murray battled to enter the law school of the all-white University of North Carolina (UNC). The effort received national attention, but Murray was not admitted to UNC, even after she sent letters to UNC's president, Frank Porter Graham, questioning why she wasn't accepted. Murray was accepted into Howard University's law school instead. Howard University was an all-black university located in Washington, D.C.

She was the only woman and the top student in her graduating class from Howard University in 1944. She was accepted into the graduate program at Howard University, but didn't want to go. She tried to enroll at Harvard University in 1944, but was rejected because of her gender. She received a second, post-graduate law degree from the University of California, and in 1946, became California's first African American deputy attorney general.

In 1951 Murray was approached by the women's division of the national Methodist Church. They wanted her to write a brief study on the laws of segregation in each state, so that churches across the nation would know what was required in each state. Her response was a book that was almost 750 pages long. Chief Counsel Thurgood Marshall called her book, *States' Laws on Race and Color*, the "bible" for civil right lawyers.

## MAKING WAVES

The feminist movement is often categorized as having three waves. The First Wave began with the suffragette movement. Women of the 19th and early 20th centuries fought for the right to vote as a way to gain political power.

The Second Wave began in the 1960s. Women of this era focused on the workplace, sexuality, family, and reproductive rights. Debates about abortion and equal pay were at the forefront.

The Third Wave is happening now. Feminists today continue to fight for these issues, and also for equal rights for women of color, women of different sexual orientations, and human rights overall.

In 1961 she earned a Doctor of Jurisprudence law degree from Yale University. She was the first African American to do so. President John F. Kennedy appointed her to his Commission on the Status of Women.

Murray worked with major civil rights leaders, including Martin Luther King Jr., but was critical of the lesser role women were allowed to play. In 1966 she cofounded the National Organization for Women (NOW) with Betty Friedan.

In 1977 Murray became the first African American woman to become an Episcopal priest. Her work behind the scenes in the fight for equal rights for women and African Americans built a strong foundation for the movements she served.

*Betty Friedan (center) led the Women's Strike for Equality in New York City in 1970. The strike called for the equal treatment of women, the repeal of anti-abortion laws, and the right to childcare.*

# Betty Friedan
## (1921–2006)

Betty Friedan loved newspapers. She wrote a column for her high school newspaper. At Smith College, she took over the campus paper and doubled the number of times it was printed. She felt a sense of loss when she had to leave journalism behind to raise a family. She wrote about how alone she felt, but newspapers and magazines did not want to publish such articles.

Friedan believed that women needed to talk about how it felt to be educated, married, and unable to work. She called it "the problem that has no name." She gave it a name in a book called *The Feminine Mystique*. It shed light on the struggles of women who felt trapped in the traditional domestic roles of wife and homemaker. Women all over the world responded powerfully to this book.

Friedan's book was the just the beginning of her activism. She cofounded the National Organization for Women (NOW). The organization lobbied for equal treatment, pay, and opportunity for women in the job market.

On the 50th anniversary of the Women's Suffrage Amendment, Friedan led the Women's Strike for Equality. The strike called for the equal treatment of women, the repeal of anti-abortion laws, and the right to childcare. Friedan's first book is still considered the catalyst for the second-wave feminist movement.

*Men are not the enemy, but the fellow victims. The real enemy is women's denigration of themselves.*

—Betty Friedan

*Gloria Steinem spoke at the Women's March on January 21, 2017, the day after the presidential inauguration, in Washington D.C. The Women's March was a worldwide protest for policies regarding human rights issues.*

# Gloria Steinem
## (1934– )

Gloria Steinem did not attend a full academic year's worth of school until she was 12 years old. During summers, her father ran a dance pavilion. In the colder months, the family traveled from town to town in a trailer while her father sold antiques to dealers across the country. This kept Steinem from getting a proper education when she was young.

Steinem's unusual childhood inspired her to take up the fight for women's rights. Steinem's mother, Ruth Nuneviller was a devoted wife who felt she had given up on her own dreams to raise a family. She experienced long periods of sadness. Seeing Ruth struggle with what she called a broken spirit, Steinem decided to help women defy society's limitations on them. She wanted women to pursue their dreams.

Steinem graduated from Smith College in 1956, where she studied government. At the time, it was an unusual choice of study for a woman. But Steinem did not want a typical life. Marriage and motherhood were not important to her. Steinem soon established a career as a writer. In 1963 she published an exposé of New York City's Playboy Club. Steinem went undercover, working as a waitress. Waitresses wore a skimpy corset, three-inch heels, bunny ears, and a tail. Her essay, "A Bunny's Tale," challenged beauty standards, addressed sexual harassment, and revealed the backbreaking, low-wage work of bunnies at this glamorous club.

Steinem continued to report on women's issues and became politically active in support of feminism. In 1971 she helped found the National Women's Political Caucus. And in 1972, she cofounded *Ms.* magazine. The first issue featured Wonder Woman on its cover as a salute to female empowerment. The magazine reported on issues such as domestic violence, abortion, and women in prison.

Steinem continues to speak out about women's issues. She delivers speeches about equality all over the world and organizes women's feminist events.

*Wangari Maathai, 2005*

# Wangari Maathai
## (1940–2011)

Near Wangari Maathai's home in Nyeri, Kenya, there was a clear stream where her family drew water for drinking, washing, and gardening. She remembers spying clusters of clear frog eggs in that stream. But when she returned to her home after college, 10 years later, the stream had dried up, as had many other natural resources in her homeland.

Maathai had earned a degree in biology from Mount St. Scholastica College in Atchison, Kansas. She also earned an MS degree from the University of Pittsburgh and a PhD in Veterinary Medicine from the University of Nairobi. She understood that her country's economic future flowed from its natural resources. She saw that years of deforestation had robbed Kenya of its rivers and crops. She and a small group of women began planting trees. They started with seven trees. The movement grew. Maathai traveled throughout Kenya, encouraging women to plant trees. She explained to them, "If you destroy the forest, then the river will stop flowing, the rains will become irregular, the crops will fail, and you will die of hunger and starvation."

The women of Kenya responded and in 1977 the Green Belt Movement was established. Maathai created this movement to plant trees, generate income, and stop soil erosion. She also incorporated empowerment for women. Today, the Green Belt Movement has planted more than 51 million trees in Africa. The organization has helped more than 900,000 women.

In 2004 Maathai became the first African woman to win the Nobel Peace Prize. It was awarded for her work in sustainable development, democracy, and women's rights. In 2009 Ban Ki-moon, the United Nations secretary-general, named Maathai a UN Messenger of Peace. Maathai's mission to improve the lives of others earned her this title.

Maathai founded the Nobel Women's Initiative with six other female peace laureates to amplify the visibility of women internationally working toward peace, justice, and equality. She once said, "We are called to assist the earth to heal her wounds, and in the process, to heal our own."

As of 2017, nearly 900 people have received the Nobel Peace Prize. Only 48 have been women.

# Chapter 2

# WOMEN WHO WROTE THE TRUTH

Some women lead governments. Some women lead protests. And some fight for justice through their creative works. Essays, music, novels, and plays allow artists to explore new ideas and present them to a wide audience.

## Simone de Beauvoir
### (1908–1986)

Simone de Beauvoir was obsessed with hiking. On a typical day, she set out across the hills in Marseille, France, with a few bananas and buns in a basket. She hiked by herself. Often, she did not return for five, six, or even 10 hours. Her love of solitary walks was unusual for a woman of her era. And it was not the only unusual part of her life.

Simone de Beauvoir was raised in a strict Catholic family. For years, she planned to be a nun. She began her education in a Catholic school for girls.

*Simone de Beauvoir, 1949*

Later on, she decided to pursue and teach philosophy.

In 1929 de Beauvoir earned a degree from the prestigious Sorbonne University in Paris. As the youngest person to pass the notoriously difficult philosophy exam, she also was the youngest philosophy teacher in France.

Through her short stories, novels, and essays, Simone became famous as a feminist, philosopher, and revolutionary. She had a profound influence on the French intellectual scene. Her most famous book, *The Second Sex*, was a 1,000-page critique of male domination of women throughout history. Published in 1949, one of the main priciples of de Beauvoir's book was that growing up female made a bigger difference than people realized. Not only were there legal differences, including women not having the right to open their own bank account until 1965, but deeper differences that were experienced everyday. Simone de Beauvoir is hailed as one of the earliest and most influential of 20th century feminist thinkers.

## bell hooks
### (1952– )

When writer and activist bell hooks left her rural Kentucky home as a teenager, she did not plan to return. Hopkinsville, Kentucky was small and segregated. She was expected to be a quiet and well-behaved young woman. But she found herself talking back. She could not stay quiet about the sexism and racism she saw in her world.

She had already begun writing poetry at age 10. As she began having her work published, she felt she needed a pseudonym. She used her grandmother's name, Bell Hooks, though she decided not to capitalize it. She felt the lower case letters helped put the focus on her message instead of herself.

After graduating high school, hooks attended Stanford University in California, where she majored in English. In between her full-time studies and a job as a telephone operator, hooks started writing a book. After several drafts and lots of hard work, *Ain't I a Woman* was published in 1981. She wrote it in an easy, familiar style. The language hooks uses is not metaphoric and is easy to interpret. She wanted the language to be easy enough that people felt able to understand her poetry. In her children's books, poetry, and academic texts, she stands up for those who are overlooked by society. She is an especially fierce advocate for black women. She argues that the feminist movement often leaves them out.

*bell hooks, 1985*

Hooks has since published more than 30 books on race, gender, class, education, mass media, and feminism. She has given lectures and made appearances around the world. hooks once thought she could never go back to Kentucky. But in 2014, she founded the bell hooks Institute there. The Institute brings together scholars and thinkers to focus on race, class, and gender. And in the rich Kentucky earth, hooks plants trees and White Dawn climbing roses, a type of rose cultivated by the women in her family for generations.

## Joan Jett
### (1958– )

When Joan Jett picked up her first guitar in 1972, female rock stars were not very common. Her guitar teacher told her women could not play rock and roll. Jett was happy to prove him wrong.

She entered the music business at 15 and, in 1975, she cofounded the punk-pop band The Runaways. After The Runaways broke up in 1979 Jett struggled as a solo artist. She was rejected by more than 23 record companies. So she and producer Kenny Laguna decided to create their own label. Blackheart Records launched in 1980. This decision made her the first female rock artist to own and control an independent record company. It paved the way for the phenomenal success of her band, The Blackhearts.

Their album, *I Love Rock 'n' Roll*, released in November 1981, was an immediate hit. Jett's covers of classics, including "I Love Rock 'n' Roll" and "Crimson and Clover" were very popular. Jett's original songs, such as "Bad Reputation" and "I Hate Myself for Loving You," became classics.

*Joan Jett gave her acceptance speech after being inducted into the Rock and Roll Hall of Fame in 2015.*

Jett is widely acknowledged as an inspiration for the riot-grrrl movement of the 1990s. Around a dozen all-female punk bands pushed the idea that girls should make, distribute, and control their own art. They published gritty underground magazines to unite and empower girls during the days before the Internet. They organized meetings to help put a stop to things such as homophobia, weightism, sexism, racism, and physical and emotional violence against women.

Joan Jett was inducted into the Rock and Roll Hall of Fame in 2015.

# Alison Bechdel

## (1960– )

Alison Bechdel has marched in many political protests and demonstrations, but she also knows what it feels like to protest alone—as an artist, in her studio. Her graphic memoirs and comic strips present the experiences of lesbian women in a society that still struggles with LGBTQ rights.

Bechdel studied art in college, first at Simon's Rock College in Massachusetts, and later at Oberlin College in Ohio. Soon after she transferred to Oberlin, Bechdel came out to her parents as a lesbian. Bechdel was worried about how her parents, especially her father, might react. So she sent her parents a letter. Bruce Bechdel surprised his daughter by seeming pleased with the news. It turned out that he had had several homosexual relationships himself. Bechdel's mother, Helen, soon filed for divorce. But only a few months later, Bruce was struck by a car and killed.

After graduating from Oberlin in 1981, Bechdel began drawing comic strips. She'd drawn her first comics in the margins of letters to her friends. The publication *WomaNews* printed her first comic strip. It was called "Dykes to Watch Out For." Her comic strip soon developed a following. Two years later, it was picked up for syndication and printed in newspapers across the country. The strip was so successful that by the 1990s it became Bechdel's full-time job.

In one of the "Dykes to Watch Out For" comics, a character explains that she only goes to a movie if it meets three requirements: it must have at least two women; those women have to talk to each other; and the conversation has to be about something other than a man. The method of judging movies is now called the Bechdel test. A surprising number of popular films fail this test. It has been cited by academics and film critics as a way to judge the portrayal of women in movies.

In 1998 Bechdel began writing *Fun Home: A Family Tragicomic*. The graphic novel dealt with her relationship with her father and his death. When it was published in 2006, it met with widespread success. She followed up with *Are You My Mother?* in 2012. The next year, *Fun Home* was adapted into a stage musical. It made its Broadway debut in 2015 and was a hit. *Fun Home*

*Alison Bechdel, 2017*

won multiple Tony awards, and it was even nominated for the Pulitzer Prize. Lesbian women are not often portrayed in popular culture. Bechdel's pioneering work shows lesbian women in realistic and meaningful ways in a society in which they are often overlooked.

# Roxane Gay
## (1974– )

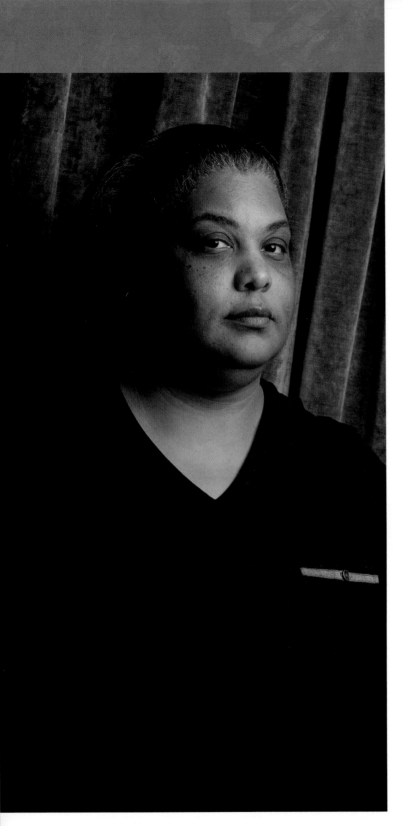

*Roxane Gay, 2016*

In *World of Wakanda*, part of Marvel Comics' Black Panther series, a highly trained, all-female fighting force called the Dora Milaje, guards the royal family. Leading the elite bodyguards are Ayo and Aneka, two black warrior women who are in a relationship with one another. For the first time in Marvel history, a series was written by an African American woman--feminist author and editor Roxane Gay.

Gay is a warrior in her own right. She is a much-loved author of books and a contributer to *The New York Times*, where she regularly wrestles with sexism, racism, and other societal problems. She earned a Master's degree in creative writing from the University of Nebraska-Lincoln and a PhD in Rhetoric and

Technical Communication at Michigan Technological University.

After her PhD was complete, Gay published a collection of short stories called *Ayiti*. In August 2014 she moved to Indiana to teach in the creative writing department at Purdue University. While there, Gay published her debut novel, *An Untamed State,* and a collection of essays called *Bad Feminist*. In 2017 a set of Gay's short stories entitled *Difficult Women*, and a memoir, *Hunger,* were published. In *Hunger,* Gay directly addressed her sexual assault as a youth and the ways she coped with it.

In all of her work, Gay fights against the stereotypes and limitations society places on women and people of color. She exposes the threats and dangers women and people of color face every day. And she tells stories that allow women and people of color to see themselves as they really are: both vulnerable and powerful.

"People want to be able to see themselves," she says. "It's just important to show a range of different ways of living and moving through the world and different kinds of bodies and different backgrounds and cultures. We're not all the same, and there's nothing wrong with that."

> **When you can't find someone to follow, you have to find a way to lead by example.**
> —Manal al-Sharif

# Chimamanda Ngozi Adichie
## (1977– )

*Chimamanda Ngozi Adichie, 2016*

The church service was over. The candles had been blown out and the smell of incense had disappeared. Chimamanda Adichie's parents waited. The other families had all gone home, but their young daughter had important questions to ask the priest, and so they waited. Their patience paid off.

Chimamanda grew up to be a novelist who asked hard questions of Nigerian society, and later, the larger world. At 19, she came to the U.S. with a scholarship to study communications at Drexel University in Philadelphia. She later graduated summa cum laude from Eastern Connecticut State University (ECSU) with degrees in communications and political science. While at ECSU, she wrote for the university literary journal and started her first novel, *Purple Hibiscus*, about Nigerian life. It was published in 2003 when she was 26. She also earned a master's degree in creative writing from Johns Hopkins University and in African studies from Yale University.

Her second novel, *Half of a Yellow Sun*, about the war in Biafra (1967–1970), a fight for freedom between Biafra and Nigeria, was published in the United Kingdom and then in the U.S.

Adichie was a fellow at Princeton University and received a fellowship that allowed her to finish her third novel, *Americanah*. It's a story about family and immigration set in Nigeria and New Jersey. Her work places the lives of women, immigrants, and people of color center stage. Focusing on their experiences is important because mainstream culture often minimizes them.

Adichie has used her fame as a writer to champion social justice and feminist causes. In 2012, Adichie gave a TED talk called, "We Should All Be Feminists," in which she explains the case for gender equality and states that both men and women should be feminists. She gave another called "The Danger of a Single Story" that encourages the acceptance of stories from many different cultures. Her talks attract millions of viewers. Using the power of her words, Adichie asks people to question the values, stereotypes, and limitations they have held sacred for too long.

*Claudia Rankine, 2014*

# Claudia Rankine
## (1963– )

The poet Claudia Rankine remembers the exact moment when something political awoke in her. In 1991 an African American man named Rodney King was pursued by police cars in Los Angeles because he was speeding. When they finally caught King, four police officers brutally beat and kicked him as other officers stood by and watched. The officers broke his bones and caused permanent brain damage—and the whole episode was captured on film. All four police officers were tried in court. Rankine remembers waiting for the verdict to be televised. And she burst into tears when she heard the words: not guilty.

"All of a sudden, I felt like an alien," she said. "I don't think I understood or felt as vulnerable ever before. Because I think I always sort of believed in the justice system before that, even though I knew its history."

Rankine was born in Kingston, Jamaica, and moved to the U.S. when she was seven years old. After graduating first with a bachelor's degree from Williams College in Massachusetts and then from Columbia University with a master's degree in poetry, she published five volumes of poetry and several plays. In addition, she edited several collections of essays and poems. Her poems lace images and words together. And in much of her work, she has confronted the problem of racism in the U.S.

Her most famous volume of poetry, *Citizen*, shares a collection of encounters in which white people say or do something that demeans a black person. The individual encounters pile up. After a while, readers get a sense of the exhaustion that people of color experience in a racist culture. She is unafraid to write about the mourning and fear that come from living in a country where slavery, lynching, poverty, and police brutality have threatened black lives for centuries.

Rankine's poems are beautiful even when the subjects they explore are painful. For her daring work, she has been awarded the Los Angeles Book Award, a Guggenheim fellowship, and a MacArthur Genius Grant, among many other awards.

# Chapter 3

# WOMEN WHO SPOKE TRUTH TO POWER

Challenging powerful people or laws can be a dangerous thing. But there are some women who did speak their truths, often at great risk to their safety. They are some of the bravest women in the world. Their efforts changed minds, changed laws, and changed cultures for the better.

## Sojourner Truth
### (1797–1883)

Few women in U.S. history have spoken truth to so many different powers as Sojourner Truth. She challenged the man who enslaved her and then went back on his promise to free her. She stood before a judge and argued to keep her five-year-old son. And she gave a powerful speech to a women's rights convention, saying black women deserved the vote as much as white women.

Born into slavery under the name Isabella in 1797, Sojourner Truth was subjected to violence and cruelty so severe that she had to escape with only her baby

*Sojourner Truth, 1864*

daughter, Sophia. With the help of an abolitionist couple, the Van Wagenans, she won custody of her son, Peter, from a plantation owner. She was the first black woman to take on a white man in court and win.

Truth had a profound religious experience and became a Methodist. She began traveling as an abolitionist preacher, saying: "The Spirit calls me, and I must go." During this time, she dictated stories to Olive Gilbert, who wrote them into a book titled *The Narrative of Sojourner Truth: A Northern Slave.*

Truth is most well known for "Ain't I A Woman?," a feminist, abolitionist speech she gave during the Ohio Women's Rights Convention of 1851. This speech called for the equal treatment of women and black citizens. It was a controversial opinion at the time. She spoke many more times at

other conventions, and also traveled to recruit black soldiers for the Union Army. She worked hard to improve the lives of people who had been freed— even leading a campaign to persuade Congress to give land to people who had been enslaved. She remains a towering figure among those who fought for freedom and equal rights for African Americans and women.

## Rosa Parks
### (1913–2005)

Rosa Parks had seen this bus driver before. James Blake had a habit of asking African American passengers to pay their fares at the front of the bus, then telling them to get off and re-enter through the back doors. When they stepped off, he'd roar away, leaving them in a cloud of fumes. When Rosa Parks saw Blake, she suspected trouble. And she decided that

*Rosa Parks (center) was one of the first people to ride the newly desegregated buses in Montgomery, Alabama in 1956.*

day was the time to fight back.

Rosa Parks came from a family of activists. Her parents were former slaves and strong advocates for racial equality. When she was 30, she became active in the

National Association for the Advancement of Colored People (NAACP). The organization fought the unfair segregation laws in southern states.

In 1955 Parks and the NAACP heard

about a teenager named Claudette Colvin who refused to leave her seat at the front of a bus in Montgomery, Alabama. Parks was inspired by Colvin's resistance. On December 1 of that year, after Parks left her job as a seamstress, she took a seat in the middle of the bus. Parks was asked to stand and give up her seat for a white man because the front of the bus seats were already taken, but she refused. The bus driver called the police and had Parks arrested.

The NAACP took the story to the papers. They organized a boycott of the Montgomery buses. On December 5 Parks was found guilty of violating the segregation laws. But this unfair policy angered the black citizens of Montgomery. Black people boycotted the buses. They walked, carpooled, and took taxis instead. They remained committed to the cause. The Montgomery bus boycott lasted 381 days. With steep financial losses mounting, Montgomery had no choice but to lift its segregation laws on public buses.

Parks suffered for her role in the boycott. She and her husband lost their jobs. Facing regular threats against their lives, they eventually moved to Detroit, Michigan. Parks took a job at the Detroit office of Congressman John Conyers Jr. She continued to support civil rights causes and is celebrated today as one of the most important inspirations in the Civil Rights movement.

In 1956 the U.S. District Court ruled that segregation on Montgomery, Alabama, buses was unconstitutional, or citing the Supreme Court's decision in *Brown v. Board of Education.*

# Barbara Walters
## (1929– )

The scene: a trendy night club called the Latin Quarter. A parade of performers—musical artists such as Frank Sinatra and movie stars including Mae West—stroll through the club. Up in the lighting booth, the daughter of the club's owner sits in a corner reading a book. She is used to the celebrities. Fast forward a few decades, and Barbara Walters is once again surrounded by the rich and famous. This time she gives them her full attention, because they are on her show, *20/20*.

Walters graduated from Sarah Lawrence College in 1953 with a degree in English. She first worked as a secretary and then got a job at WRCA-TV, where she developed skills in research, writing, and production. In 1974 Walters co-hosted NBC's *Today Show*, where she resisted pressure to focus on light-hearted stories aimed at women. In 1962 she pushed for an assignment that would take her to India and Pakistan with first lady Jacqueline Kennedy. In 1972 Walters was one of the journalists chosen to accompany President Nixon on his trip to China.

*Barbara Walters, 2008*

In 1976 Walters became the first woman to co-anchor the evening news. She signed a contract with *ABC World News Tonight*, making her the highest-paid woman in the industry. Her annual salary was $1 million. Walters won a total of 13 Emmy Awards. She also won a Peabody award for a *20/20* episode.

A sharp and perceptive reporter, Walters interviewed every U.S. president and first lady from Richard and Pat Nixon through Barack and Michelle Obama. She's also known for interviews with Colin Powell, Fidel Castro, and Katharine Hepburn, and a joint interview with Israeli Prime Minister Menachem Begin and Egyptian President Anwar Sadat. She never shied away from asking tough questions.

From 1997 to 2014 Walters cohosted *The View*. After a career spanning five decades, Walters retired in 2014, but continued her annual "Most Fascinating People" interviews into 2015. Her pioneering work broke glass ceilings in the television industry. Because she fought so hard to be taken seriously as a journalist, she made the path smoother for female journalists of the next generation.

## Charlene Teters
### (1952– )

When the University of Illinois offered Charlene Teters a spot in its graduate arts program, she felt an immense sense of honor. She had already earned a bachelor's degree in art from the College of Santa Fe, New Mexico. As a member of the Spokane Tribe, she was selected because her art celebrated her American Indian heritage. But when she arrived at the Urbana-Champaign campus, she was surrounded by negative images of an American Indian chief on clothing, cups , and even on toilet paper.

Then she attended a sports game where a white student impersonated an American Indian chief. The student mascot performed a disrespectful dance. Teters was deeply disturbed by the show. In response, she began silently standing outside sporting events, holding a sign that read, "American Indians are human not mascots." She became vice president of the National Coalition on Racism in Sports and the Media. The organization aims to convince sports teams, particularly in universities, that the use of American Indian stereotypes as mascots is wrong. Additionally, they want to remove any misuse of American Indian symbols. Teters' commitment to

*Charlene Teters, 2011*

her work led her to be named "Person of the Week" in 1997 by Peter Jennings on *ABC World News Tonight*.

Teters' other work includes serving as senior editor of *Native Artist* magazine and the Hugh O. LaBounty Endowed Chair of Interdisciplinary Knowledge at California State Polytechnic University. She was the first ever Artist in Residence at the American Museum of Natural

## MASCOT CONTROVERSY

Many sports teams have used American Indian words and images as their names and mascots. The Washington Redskins are one of the most well known. Indigenous people point out that the term is an offensive slur. However, team owner Dan Snyder says he will never change the name, which he believes conveys honor, respect, and pride. And many longtime fans oppose a change as well. They don't see the name as being offensive and would prefer that the team they have been following stay the same.

More general terms such as "Chiefs," "Braves," and "Warriors" are also controversial. These names are used not just in professional sports, but in high school and little league teams all across the country.

# Sylvia Tamale
## (1967– )

In 2003 the largest newspaper in Uganda, *The New Vision*, asked readers a question: Who was the worst woman in the country? Their answer: Sylvia Tamale. She had dared to speak out against traditional African values. She had stood up for equal rights for women and for the LGBTQ citizens of Uganda. That made her a threat to the established way of life many people wanted to preserve.

How did Tamale respond to the announcement? She became "a smiling duck," she says. She allowed the insult to roll off her back, and she kept fighting for equal treatment for all of Uganda's people.

History in New York City. She currently lives in Santa Fe, New Mexico, where she is the Professor of Art at the Institute of American Indian Arts. A PBS documentary film about her activism called her the "Rosa Parks of Native Americans."

At the time of the newspaper poll, Tamale was a professor at Makerere University, the most respected university in the country. Before that, Tamale received a Bachelor of Laws, and proceeded to Harvard Law School to earn a Master of Laws. In 1997, she received her PhD in Sociology and Feminist Studies from the University of Minnesota.

In 2000 Tamale published her first book, *When Hens Begin to Crow: Gender and Parliamentary Politics in Uganda*. She wrote academic papers and news articles. She spoke at political gatherings and in the media. Above all, she used her university position to educate the students who would lead future generations. She spoke up for those who she felt had no voice: gay and lesbian people, women who experience domestic violence,

*Sylvia Tamale, 2010*

refugees, and female students who have experienced sexual violence on campus.

In 2004 she became the first woman to serve as dean of the Faculty of Law at Makerere University. Tamale stayed in this position until 2008. She was also a member of the University Senate, where she pushed the school to implement a sexual harassment policy. Makerere became one of the first African colleges to enforce such a policy. Many other African universities followed this example. Tamale has come to be viewed as a leading feminist scholar.

# Caryl Churchill
## (1938– )

When the lights dim and the curtain rises, the members of a theater audience become witnesses to the world on stage. If the play is very good, they may leave the theater feeling different from when they entered it. They may view their own lives, and the world at large, in a new way. Having witnessed problems and possibilities, those who watch feel empowered to become the ones who change things. British dramatist Caryl Churchill has spent her life creating plays that artfully expose the problems women face in society.

Her career as a playwright began while she was studying English literature at Lady Margaret Hall, a women's college at the University of Oxford. While she was there, she wrote her first three plays—*Downstairs, Having a Wonderful Time,* and *Easy Death.* All three plays were produced and performed by Oxford's theatrical troupes, and *Downstairs,* her first play, received an award at the *Sunday Times* National Union of Students Drama Festival. Churchill graduated in 1960 and stayed in London.

Throughout the 1960s and 1970s she wrote radio and television plays for the BBC network. In 1974 Churchill became the first woman to be named Resident Dramatist at the Royal Court Theater.

Churchill's many plays challenge accepted roles for women. They expose the ways in which society trains men to dominate women and one race to dominate another. Her work shows how people can defy unfair treatment and expectations. Because her plays often have innovative forms, they awaken audiences to new possibilities, both in theater and in society.

Churchill has received three Obie Awards, a Society of West End Theatre Award, the Laurence Olivier/ BBC Award for Best New Play, the Richard Hillary Memorial Prize, and the *Evening Standard* Award for Best Comedy of the Year. In 2010 Churchill was inducted into the American Theater Hall of Fame.

*Caryl Churchill, 1983*

# Chapter 4

# WOMEN TO WATCH

Watch out, world!

These young women are part of a new generation of social justice warriors. They are challenging inequality and working to improve living and working conditions for people around the world.

## Alicia Garza
### (1981– )

Like millions of Americans, social justice warrior Alicia Garza was waiting for the verdict. An unarmed African American boy had been murdered, and it seemed the whole nation awaited the outcome of his killer's trial. Then came the news: not guilty. No one would be held accountable for the death of Trayvon Martin.

Garza said she felt "punched in the gut" by the verdict. It echoed the thousands of times in U.S. history when young black men were killed by white people without any penalty. She poured

*Alicia Garza, 2016*

out her emotions on Facebook, using the now-famous words "Black lives matter." The words caught on. Across the nation, outraged people protested and spoke up about the need to stop violence against African American people. Because of this Garza, along with Patrisse Cullors and Opal Tometi, harnessed the anger and started the Black Lives Matter movement to improve the lives of African Americans.

Garza's activism began in her home state of California, where she was the director of People Organized To Win Employment Rights in the San Francisco Bay area. There, she fought against the trend of gentrification. Gentrification is what happens when wealthy people buy homes in city neighborhoods where low-income families live. This trend drives up the cost of housing and forces poor families out of the area.

Garza has also fought against the use of excessive force by police officers. In 2014 a young African American man named Michael Brown was shot and killed by a white police officer. It was one in a series of incidents in which police killed African Americans based on suspicion, not evidence. Brown's body was left on the street in Ferguson, Missouri, for four and a half hours. When no one was held accountable for his death, people protested nationwide. Garza led a protest to stop the San Francisco subway for four and a half hours, the amount of time Michael Brown lay in the street. Garza also led the Freedom Ride to Ferguson, Missouri, which launched Black Lives Matter chapters across the country.

Today, more than 20 Black Lives Matter chapters intervene to stop violence against black people worldwide.

> *I believe a society will not be free if the women of that society are not free.*
>
> —Manal al-Sharif

## Manal al-Sharif
### (1979– )

Manal al-Sharif was arrested, strip-searched, and jailed. When she was released, she lost her job. She endured death threats. And she was forced to leave the country of her birth. What crime brought such punishment upon her? She dared to drive a car in Saudi Arabia.

In 2011 it was against the law for a woman to drive without a license, and women

*Manal al-Sharif, 2012*

were not allowed to be issued licenses. Nevertheless, al-Sharif got behind the wheel and drove. She did it as a form of protest. She filmed her act of defiant driving and uploaded it to the Internet. Within hours, hundreds of thousands of people watched her.

Al-Sharif had already done a lot. With her father's permission, she had studied computer science at King Abdulaziz University. She would not have been able to study there without his permission. In 2002 she began working for the national oil company, Aramco. Women were permitted to drive within the company's compound, so al-Sharif's brother gave her lessons. She married a coworker and had a son, but her husband was abusive. They divorced after he insisted she stop working. In Saudi Arabia, fathers receive custody of children after a divorce.

In 2009 al-Sharif went to the United States on a work exchange program. She received her driver's license and rented her own apartment. Returning to Saudi Arabia a year later, she wanted to fight for more freedom for women. In 2011 she learned that the ban on women driving was not a law but that women were banned from getting drivers' licenses, which meant they couldn't drive legally. That's when she defied the law and filmed herself driving.

She urged Saudi women with international licenses to drive on June 17, which she declared "Women2Drive Day." But before Women2Drive Day, al-Sharif was arrested and imprisoned. The news sparked international demand for her release. She was freed after nine days.

Al-Sharif has since remarried. She has another son and lives in Australia. She has not been able to see her first child, and her two sons have never met. In 2017 her memoir, *Daring to Drive*, was published. In June 2018 Saudi King Salman agreed to allow women to drive.

# Janet Mock
## (1983– )

Janet Mock remembers a small crisis in kindergarten. The children were supposed to put their shoes in their cubbies. Her cubby was blue. The name on it said "Charles." But for Janet, that cubby was a mistake. She wanted to erase the word "Charles" and write a girl's name in its place. But she was convinced, even

*Janet Mock, 2016*

## TRANSGENDER IDENTITIES

Transgender people do not identify with the sex they were assigned at birth. A transgender person may identify as a woman, though she was born with male genitalia. Some transgender people do not identify as a man or a woman. They may call themselves non-binary, because they do not feel they belong at either end of the gender spectrum.

Transgender people often express their gender outwardly in their appearance with the clothes and hairstyles they wear. They may also decide to change their bodies with medication or surgery.

Transgender people often face discrimination and violence. They are more likely to be homeless, live in poverty, and take their own lives. With more people taking the lead to stand up and be their true selves, transgender people may face less discrimination.

at five years old, that wanting such a thing was wrong. Named Charles by her parents, she always identified as female. By the age of 15, Charles was insisting that everyone call her Janet. With her mother's support, she began hormone treatments. At 18 she traveled to Thailand to undergo surgery. Doctors there could change her body so that it reflected the gender with which she identified.

With the surgery behind her, Janet attended the University of Hawaii and then earned a master's degree in journalism from New York University. Mock launched her media career at *People* magazine. She worked as an editor there for five years. Today, she is a producer, TV host, and contributing editor and columnist for *Allure* magazine. She focuses on gender, race, and intersectionality. Mock describes herself as "a feminist intent on tackling stigma through storytelling."

In 2014, she also released her autobiography, *Redefining Realness: My Path to Womanhood, Identity, Love & So Much More.* It is considered the first book to be written from the perspective of a young trans person. In 2017, she wrote a follow-up, *Surpassing Certainty: What My Twenties Taught Me.*

*TIME* magazine named her one of "the most influential people on the Internet" and one of "12 new faces of black leadership." In January 2017 Mock addressed the Women's March on Washington. She called for a women's movement that included every woman.

*Owning who we are is power. Yes. We've got to dare to stand out.*

–Janet Mock

*Laura Bates, 2015*

# Laura Bates
## (1986– )

She wanted to be an actor. It was the career she had studied and practiced and prepared for. After receiving a master's degree in English literature from the University of Cambridge, Laura Bates moved to London to pursue that dream. But while she was going about her everyday work, she began noticing the sexist treatment of women. Degrading comments. Street harassment. Unwanted groping. When Bates shared her experiences, others were often dismissive and told her to not take things so seriously.

This did not change her mind about sexism, but rather proved to her how normal it had become.

Bates' frustration sparked the idea for the Everyday Sexism Project, an online resource where women and girls can share their own stories of harassment and assault. Launched without any publicity or funding, Bates hoped to collect 100 entries. By its one-year anniversary, she had received almost 25,000. The project has grown to raise awareness about sexism and provides an outlet for women to share their experiences by submitting through the website, email, or Twitter.

In 2014, Bates' first book, *Everyday Sexism*, was published. Her second, *Girl Up*, an empowering survival guide for females, came out in 2016. The Everyday Sexism Project has spread across 25 countries and currently has more than 282,000 Twitter followers. Because the following is so large, it has begun changing cultural sexism in small but powerful ways. One example: When iTunes recently offered a cosmetic surgery app to girls, Bates' followers spoke up about it and the company took down the app. Though Bates has endured threats and harassment online, the Everyday Sexism Project continues to give girls and women a space to speak out and stand together.

*Women who lead, read.*
–Laura Bates

# Emma Watson
## (1990– )

*Emma Watson, 2017*

At nine years old, Emma Watson became a witch. Not just any witch. She became Hermione Granger, possibly the most famous witch in the world. But she discovered powers of another kind in her 20s, after the Harry Potter movie series was complete. Watson discovered her ability to change the lives of women around the world by becoming a human rights activist.

She knew quite early—when she was six years old—that she wanted to act. She attended Stagecoach Theatre Arts school, a part-time theatre school in Oxford, England, where she studied singing, dancing, and acting. When her first film, *Harry Potter and the Sorcerer's Stone*, was released in November 2001, she won the Young Artist Award for Leading Young Actress in a Feature Film.

In 2009 she began her college education at Brown University in Providence, Rhode Island. That same year, she began her work as an activist with People Tree, a fashion label that promotes fair trade.

In 2014 she was appointed a United Nations Women Goodwill Ambassador. She spoke about gender inequality at the UN General Assembly to promote the launch of HeForShe, a campaign that encourages men to stand up for gender equality. Since Watson announced the campaign, more than 1.6 million men and boys have signed on to a list of specific commitments aimed at ending gender inequality.

As ambassador, she has traveled to Uruguay to encourage young women to vote and to Malawi to help end child marriage. In 2016 she launched the feminist book club "Our Shared Shelf" to raise awareness of gender equality by discussing books and articles. In 2018 she and several other actors walked the red carpet at the Golden Globe awards with fellow women's rights activists as their dates. Watson walked with Marai Larasi, director of the UK-based organization IMKAAN. IMKAAN is a feminist organization that fights violence against girls and women.

Watson continues to gain acclaim for her work as an actor and uses her platform to improve the lives of women around the globe.

> **I don't want other people to decide what I am. I want to decide that for myself.**
> —Emma Watson

# Malala Yousafzai
## (1997– )

In 2014 Malala Yousafzai became the youngest person ever to receive a Nobel Peace Prize.

"oh my lord, equip me with knowledge"

These words adorned the crest of the small school run by Malala Yousafzai's father in Mingora, Pakistan. Inside its walls, girls studied and laughed together. But in 2007 Taliban militants took control of the region and banned girls from attending school. In September 2008, after the Taliban began attacking girls' schools, Malala gave a speech at a local press club in Peshawar, entitled "How dare the Taliban take away my basic right to education?" She was 11.

The following year, she blogged for the BBC network about life under the Taliban. She used the pseudonym Gul Makai, but her identity was soon revealed. She was also the subject of a documentary, "Class Dismissed," produced by *The New York Times*. She continued to speak out and, in 2011, received Pakistan's National Youth Peace Prize and was nominated for the International Children's Peace Prize.

On October 9, 2012, she was riding the school bus home. A masked gunman boarded the bus and shot her and some of her fellow students. Malala, in critical condition, was flown to a military hospital in Peshawar. She and her family then relocated to Birmingham, England, for additional surgeries. Remarkably, she suffered no brain damage. She began attending school in Birmingham.

Malala and her father established the Malala Fund in 2013. The organization "champions every girl's right to 12 years of free, safe, quality education." That year she addressed the United Nations and published her first book, *I Am Malala*.

In October 2014 she was awarded the Nobel Peace Prize, along with Indian children's rights activist Kailash Satyarthi. At 17 years old Malala was the youngest person to receive a Nobel. In 2017 she was named a UN Messenger of Peace—again, the youngest ever.

She entered Oxford University in October 2017. She is studying philosophy, politics, and economics.

# Timeline

**1851** Sojourner Truth delivers her famous "Ain't I a Woman?" speech

**1869** Susan B. Anthony co-founds the National Woman's Suffrage Association

**1939** Pauli Murray campaigns for entry into the all-white University of North Carolina

**1945** Eleanor Roosevelt is appointed a delegate to the United Nations General Assembly

**1949** Simone de Beauvoir's *The Second Sex* is published

**1955** Rosa Parks refuses to give up her seat on the bus to a white man, sparking the Montgomery bus boycott

**1963** Betty Friedan's *The Feminine Mystique* is published

**1972** Gloria Steinem cofounds *Ms.* magazine

**1974** Caryl Churchill writes her play *Objections to Sex and Violence*

**1979** Barbara Walters begins working at *20/20* as a cohost and producer

**1991** Charlene Teters helps found the National Coalition on Racism in Sports and the Media

**2003** Sylvia Tamale is recognized as the "Worst Woman of the Year" in Uganda because of her progressive politics

**2004** Wangari Maathai becomes the first woman to win the Nobel Peace Prize

**2011** Janet Mock tells her story of being a transgender woman of color to *Marie Claire*

**2011** Manal al-Sharif declares June 17 "Woman2Drive Day" in Saudi Arabia

**2012** Laura Bates founds the Everyday Sexism Project

**2012** Chimamanda Ngozi Adichie delivers a popular TED Talk titled "We Should All Be Feminists"

**2013** Alicia Garza cofounds Black Lives Matter

**2014** Roxane Gay's essay collection *Bad Feminist* is published

**2014** Emma Watson launches her United Nations campaign HeForShe

**2014** Malala Yousafzai is awarded the Nobel Peace Prize

# Glossary

**deforestation**—to remove or cut down trees

**empower**—to supply someone with confidence or an ability

**fair trade**—trade in which fair prices are paid to producers in developing countries

**harassment**—aggressive, unwanted actions that create hostile situations

**indigenous**—native to a place

**intersectionality**—the way gender, race, and culture interact

**lobby**—to try to persuade government officials to act or vote in a certain way

**pseudonym**—a fictitious name or pen name

**Quaker**— members of a religion called the Society of Friends that opposed slavery and violence

**repeal**—to officially cancel something, such as a law

**segregation**—practice of separating people of different races, income classes, or ethnic groups

**sexism**—discrimination based on whether a person is male or female

**suffrage**—the right to vote

**temperance**—reform movement that worked to outlaw the sale and consumption of alcoholic beverages, which were blamed for a host of social problems

**transgender**— a person whose gender identity differs from their assigned sex

# Critical Thinking Questions

1. What are some of the issues that are most important to feminists? Which do you think should get the most attention? Why?
2. Should equal rights based on gender be guaranteed in the U.S. Constitution? Why or why not? Support your answer with information from the text and other sources.
3. The feminists of earlier times helped women win the right to vote and work. Do you think women and men are treated equally? If so, support your answer. If not, say some ways in which you think they are not and what might be done about that.

# Further Reading

**Favilli, Elena.** *Good Nights Stories for Rebel Girls: 100 Tales of Extraordinary Women.* New York: Timbuktu Labs, 2016.

**Schatz, Kate.** *Rad American Women A–Z: Rebels, Trailblazers, and Visionaries who Shaped Our History.* New York: City Lights Books, 2015.

**Schwartz, Heather E.** *Girls Rebel! Amazing Tales of Women Who Broke the Mold.* Girls Rock! Mankato, Minn.: Capstone Press, 2014.

# Internet Links

Use FactHound to find Internet sites related to this book.
Visit www.facthound.com
Just type in 9780756558505 and go.

# About the Author

Jill Sherman lives and writes in Brooklyn, New York. She has written dozens of books for young people. She enjoys researching new topics and is thrilled to be sharing the accomplishments of outstanding female activists with young readers. Jill is training to run a 10K and enjoys taking photos of her dog.

# Source Notes

Page 12, col. 2, line 10: Kathryn Schulz. "The Many Lives of Pauli Murray." *The New Yorker.* April 17, 2017, https://www.newyorker.com/magazine/2017/04/17/the-many-lives-of-pauli-murray

Page 15, col. 1, line 8: Debra Michals. "Betty Friedan." National Women's History Museum. 2017, www.womenshistory.org/education-resources/biographies/betty-friedan

Page 17, col. 2, line 3: Elizabeth Varnell. "Gloria Steinem Knows Firsthand How the Original Playboy Bunnies Got Their Hourglass Shape." *Vogue.* September 28, 2017, https://www.vogue.com/article/playboy-bunnies-hourglass-body-gloria-steinem-hugh-hefner-death-playboy-club-new-york

Page 19, col. 2, line 11: Jeffrey Gettleman. "Wangari Maathai, Nobel Peace Prize Laureate, Dies at 71." *The New York Times.* September 26, 2011, https://www.nytimes.com/2011/09/27/world/africa/wangari-maathai-nobel-peace-prize-laureate-dies-at-71.html?mtrref=www.google.com

Page 24, col. 1, line 7: "bell hooks." *Encyclopaedia Britannica.* https://www.britannica.com/biography/bell-hooks

Page 23, col. 1, line 18: Josephine Liptrott. "Biography: bell hooks – Author, Activist." The Heroine Collective. March 16, 2016, http://www.theheroinecollective.com/bell-hooks/

Page 37, col. 2, line 1: "Rosa Parks Biography." Biography. February 27, 2018, https://www.biography.com/people/rosa-parks-9433715

Page 38, col. 2, line 10: "Rosa Parks." History. 2009, https://www.history.com/topics/black-history/rosa-parks

Page 38, col. 1, line 6: Jeanne Theoharis. "How History Got the Rosa Parks Story Wrong." *The Washington Post.* December 1, 2015, https://www.washingtonpost.com/posteverything/wp/2015/12/01/how-history-got-the-rosa-parks-story-wrong/?noredirect=on&utm_term=.e6339ab3e3c4

Page 42, col. 1, line 3: Erik Brady. "The Real History of Native American Team Names." *USA Today.* August 24, 2016, https://www.usatoday.com/story/sports/2016/08/24/real-history-native-american-team-names/89259596/

Page 42, col. 2, line 6: ""Worst Woman of the Year": Sylvia Tamale Publishes African Sexualities." AWID Women's Rights. October 10, 2011, https://www.awid.org/news-and-analysis/worst-woman-year-sylvia-tamale-publishes-african-sexualities-reader

Page 43, col. 1, line 12: Gumisiriza Mwesigye. "Tamale: A Passionate Human Rights Activist." *Daily Monitor.* April 28, 2012, http://www.monitor.co.ug/SpecialReports/ugandaat50/1370466-1394360-14ekh7r/index.html

Page 44, col. 2, line 18: "Caryl Lesley Churchill Biography." Biography. October 16, 2014, https://www.biography.com/people/caryl-lesley-churchill-9248036

All Internet sites were accessed on May 22, 2018.

# Index